MEXICO
the people

Bobbie Kalman

The Lands, Peoples, and Cultures Series

Crabtree Publishing Company

Toronto · Oxford · New York

The Lands, Peoples, and Cultures Series

Created by Bobbie Kalman

Editor-in-Chief
Bobbie Kalman

Writing team
Bobbie Kalman
Tammy Everts
David Schimpky
Janine Schaub

Editors
Tammy Everts
David Schimpky
Janine Schaub
Petrina Gentile

Computer design and layout
Lynda Hale
Antoinette "Cookie" DeBiasi

Illustrations
Antoinette "Cookie" DeBiasi
Karen Harrison (page 12)

Printer
Worzalla Publishing Company

Separations and film
Book Art Inc.

For Sarah Giesbrecht

Special thanks to: Jürgen Bavoni, Canadian International Development Agency, Monique Denis, Antonia de Sousa-Shields, Irene Herrera (who appears on the cover), Library of Congress, Anne McLean, Pueblito Canada, Laurie Taylor, and Pierre Vachon

Photographs

Jürgen Bavoni: pages 9 (top left, bottom right), 10, 14 (top left), 17 (middle, bottom), 18 (right), 20-21, 23 (bottom), 24 (top), 27 (bottom)
Jim Bryant: pages 3, 4, 5, 9 (bottom left), 13 (bottom right), 14 (bottom left), 18 (left), 19 (left), 20 (top and inset), 26, 27 (top right), 30
CIDA/David Barbour: pages 11 (bottom), 19 (right), 23 (top left), 27 (circle)
Peter Crabtree and Bobbie Kalman: cover, title page, pages 8 (right), 11 (top), 13 (bottom left), 14 (top right, bottom right), 24 (middle, bottom), 25 (top), 26 (circle)
Richard Emblin: pages 9 (top right), 13 (top right)
James Kamstra: pages 7, 8 (middle, left), 12 (bottom), 17 (top), 23 (circle)
Diane Payton Majumdar: pages 16, 23 (top right)
Pueblito Canada: page 11 (middle)
Jean Robertson: page 25 (bottom)

Published by
Crabtree Publishing Company

350 Fifth Avenue	360 York Road, RR 4,	73 Lime Walk
Suite 3308	Niagara-on-the-Lake,	Headington
New York	Ontario, Canada	Oxford OX3 7AD
N.Y. 10118	L0S 1J0	United Kingdom

Cataloguing in Publication Data

Kalman, Bobbie, 1947-
   Mexico: the people

(Lands, Peoples, and Cultures Series)
Includes index.
ISBN 0-86505-215-8 (library bound) ISBN 0-86505-295-6 (pbk.)
This book looks at the way of life of Mexican people, including family life, education, religion, city and village life, and work.

1. Mexico - Social conditions - Juvenile literature.
I. Title. II. Series.

HN113.5.K35 1993   j972   LC 93-34764

Contents

An ancient heritage

The history of Mexico's people goes back thousands of years. The first inhabitants of Mexico were the Native peoples. The Olmecs, Zapotecs, Maya, and Aztecs were just some of these. Some groups developed into advanced societies, or **civilizations**, that accomplished a great deal in the areas of arts and sciences. These civilizations did not always develop on their own. People learned from one another and from the civilizations that had come before. The Spanish conquered the Native peoples in the sixteenth century and ruled Mexico for hundreds of years. The people of Mexico are descendants of these different groups.

The Olmecs

The Olmecs were the first great civilization in Mexico. They established many cities along the eastern coast and exchanged goods with other groups of Native peoples. They spread their religious beliefs, which focused on a mysterious god that was part human and part jaguar.

The Zapotecs

Large cities, filled with temples and pyramids, were built across southern Mexico by the Zapotec civilization. Although they were fierce warriors, the Zapotecs had an advanced culture. They studied the stars and planets and developed the first writing system in the Americas. Using **hieroglyphs**, or word-pictures, they recorded their history on stone tablets.

Teotihuacán

By about AD 400, central Mexico was controlled by the city of Teotihuacán. This metropolis was home to more than 150,000 people! Religion was an important part of life in Teotihuacán. Thousands of priests performed ceremonies in the city's many temples. Missionaries were sent out to spread their beliefs to other peoples. Today, experts do not know what the residents of Teotihuacán called themselves. The name was never recorded, nor was it remembered by the people who followed.

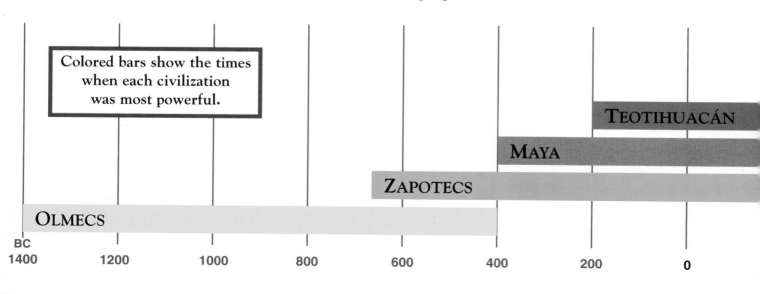

Colored bars show the times when each civilization was most powerful.

TEOTIHUACÁN | MAYA | ZAPOTECS | OLMECS

BC 1400 | 1200 | 1000 | 800 | 600 | 400 | 200 | 0

The amazing Maya

Around the time of Teotihuacán, the Mayan civilization had spread across southern Mexico and Central America. The remarkable Maya recorded their history, built majestic cities, and were expert astronomers and mathematicians. The Mayan cities traded food, tools, and other goods with one another.

The Mayan civilization declined around AD 900. The huge cities were deserted and fell into ruin. No one knows for certain why this great civilization declined. Some experts believe that hurricanes, earthquakes, disease, or war may have been responsible. Recently, several ancient Mayan ruins were discovered in the rainforests of Belize and Guatemala. It is believed that these findings may shed light on the mystery of the Mayan decline.

Aztec civilization

Around AD 1300, another great civilization emerged in central Mexico. The Aztecs were powerful warriors who conquered neighboring peoples. The capital of their empire was the city of Tenochtitlán. This amazing city featured bridges, canals, and huge pyramids.

The Spanish

The Aztec civilization lasted until the Spanish came to America. The Spanish changed life in Mexico. They destroyed the Native civilizations and introduced European beliefs and culture to Mexico's people.

(above) Large groups of Maya still live in southern Mexico. This young boy and his family practice many traditions of the ancient Maya.
(opposite page) The Temple of Quetzalcoatl in Teotihuacán honored a god who gave the people corn.

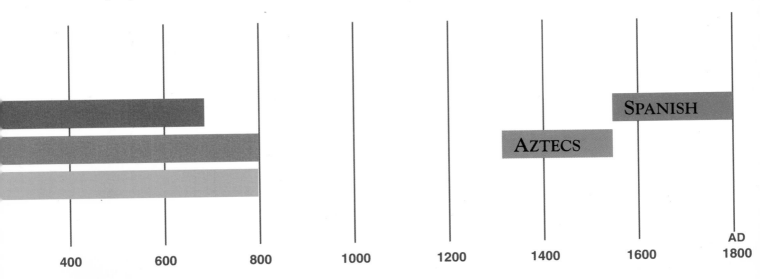

The Maya

Class system

The Mayan society of long ago had a **class system** consisting of the ruling class, nobles, workers, farmers, and slaves. A person's class determined his or her job, dwelling place, and marriage partner.

The rulers were the most important people. They were religious and political leaders who lived in spacious castles inside the cities. The nobles lived in the cities and helped the rulers. The homes of the workers were in the city suburbs, whereas the farmers resided in the countryside surrounding the city. The slaves served the rulers and nobles in the cities.

Living off the land

Like most farming peoples, the Maya loved the land. Every stage of farming—from plowing to planting to harvesting—was combined with a religious ceremony that included offering food, prayers, and human sacrifices to the gods. The Maya also hunted for food. Using bows and arrows, traps, nets, and spears, they captured deer, wild boars, rabbits, and turkeys. It is believed that they trained dogs to help in the hunt. The Maya kept bees, which provided them with honey and wax. The people who lived near water caught fish, shellfish, and turtles for food.

The family

Mayan men and women married when they were still teenagers. After the wedding, the couple moved in with the wife's family for up to six years. When the six years were up, the married couple lived near or with the husband's family for the rest of their lives. Mothers were very strict with their daughters and taught them all the skills they would need as future wives. Fathers trained sons to hunt and farm. When women died, they passed their belongings on to their daughters. Mayan men passed their property down to their sons.

A warlike people

At one time, experts believed that the Maya were a peaceful people. Today, many think that the Maya were actually very warlike. Fights between cities were common. Some cities had high stone walls and moats to keep out invaders. Mayan farmers were part-time soldiers who fought when they were needed. They used weapons such as bows, arrows, spears, clubs, and daggers. One unusual Mayan weapon was the **hornet bomb**, a hornet nest thrown at enemies during battle. Ouch! Nobody knows how the Maya gathered and stored these weapons without getting stung.

(above) Mayan cities were the centers of Mayan life and culture. Outside the cities, farmers grew food for the rulers and nobles. Farm families led simple lives. They lived in plain, wooden homes with thatched roofs. While the men toiled in the fields, women did work such as washing clothing in rivers and streams. *(right)* The ways of the ancient Maya have been preserved by the modern Maya. This young woman grinds corn into meal and makes tortillas in the same way Mayan women have for centuries.

Each year on October 12, Mexicans celebrate their mixture of peoples, races, and cultures in a holiday called the Day of the Race. People may be *criollo*, *mestizo*, mulatto, or of Native origin, but they all consider themselves Mexican first.

Mestizos

Seven out of ten Mexicans are *mestizos*, which means that they have mixed Native and Spanish ancestry. Some *mestizos* have very dark skin, whereas others have fair complexions.

Mulattos

During the seventeenth and eighteenth centuries, African slaves were brought to work on Mexican plantations. Many Mexicans and Africans married. Their descendants are called **mulattos**. Mulattos form only a small part of Mexico's population, but they celebrate the Day of the Race with pride.

Criollos

Criollo is the name given to Mexico's tiny population of Europeans, Americans, and Canadians. Some *criollos* are descendants of the Spanish who first arrived in Mexico. Many *criollos* have moved to Mexico to enjoy the beautiful weather and fascinating culture.

Native Mexicans

There are over four million true Native peoples living in Mexico today. They are just a small part of Mexico's entire population. Native Mexicans belong to over 50 groups, each with its own language and traditions. The largest groups are the Maya of the south, the Huichols of the northwest, and the Totonacs of the east. Because of poverty, many Native Mexicans have difficult lives. They rarely own the land they farm, and few are educated enough to get well-paying jobs. The Native peoples of Mexico struggle to maintain their old ways in a modern society.

 # Population explosion!

Mexico has a population of over 85 million people. Experts predict that in twenty years that number will double! Almost half of Mexico's people live on small farms in the country. Since the 1950s, many Mexicans have moved from the countryside to the city, hoping to have better lives. The population of the cities is growing quickly, but there are not enough homes, schools, and hospitals to meet the needs of every city dweller.

A country of young people

Mexico is a country of young people—one out of every three Mexicans is under fifteen years old! It is difficult for families to support so many children. Some young people must quit school to help their parents. Farm children toil long hours in the fields, whereas city children take odd jobs to earn money. Working children grow up quickly because they have many responsibilities.

Street children

About one-and-a-half million Mexican children live on the city streets. Many are orphans whose only families are gangs of other street youths. Few street children will ever have the opportunity to go to school.

Without an education, their lives are not likely to improve. Some charities are trying to help these children, but their numbers are growing along with Mexico's population.

Illegal immigration

There are not enough jobs to employ everyone in Mexico. Many Mexicans look to the United States as a place where they can earn a living. Thousands apply for legal immigrant status each year, but few are accepted. As a result, many choose to slip across the border. Most of these **illegal immigrants** are men whose families remain in Mexico. Much of the money they earn in the United States is sent home to give their families better lives.

The illegal immigration problem is a source of conflict between the United States and Mexico. The American government patrols the border and arrests thousands of illegal immigrants each year. These people are then sent back to Mexico.

(above) Schools in Mexico are becoming more and more crowded. These children are lucky to be able to attend school. Many boys and girls must quit school and take jobs to help support their families.

(above) Despite overpopulation, many young people have happy, comfortable lives.
(left) The number of homeless children in Mexico is growing. Charitable organizations help by creating schools for street children.
(below) The streets of Mexico City are often packed with people.

 # Family life

Mexican families are large and close knit. The average household consists of a father, mother, and two or three children, but aunts, uncles, and grandparents often live under the same roof, too. Weddings, birthdays, and fiestas are good opportunities for Mexican families and friends to gather together for feasting, singing, dancing, and fireworks.

Eating together

Mealtimes are important family occasions. After a busy day, family members talk with one another over dinner. Almost every home has a dining room where the entire family can sit down together. After a tasty meal, which might include guacamole, enchiladas, *fríjoles refritos* (refried beans), strong coffee, and a delicious custard flan, the family gathers around the radio or television.

Well-behaved children

Most Mexican children are happy and well behaved. They are taught to be polite, respect their elders, and work together for the good of the family. Mexican parents use a combination of firm discipline and love in raising their children. A writer named Charles Flandreau once said that all the children in the world should behave as well as Mexican children!

Coming of age

Mexican girls look forward to their fifteenth birthday. On this day, a young girl becomes a *quinceanera*, or a *señorita*—a young woman. This celebration of entering the adult world carries many privileges. A *quinceanera* is entitled to more privacy, a later bedtime, and permission to join the promenade of young people around the town square on Sunday evenings.

(top) On a Mexican girl's fifteenth birthday, a **mariachi** *band wakes her with music and singing.*
(bottom) Despite greater awareness of women's rights, housework is the responsibility of Mexican women.

Parental duties

In a traditional Mexican household, the mother cooks, cleans, and looks after the health and welfare of the family, even if she has a job outside the home. The father is the head of the family. He earns most of the money and makes the important decisions. The decision-making process is not as simple as it seems. Though the father announces the decisions, he and his wife have usually discussed them beforehand.

The changing roles of women

Mexico is a nation that is known for the *machismo* of its men. *Machismo* is the word used to describe aggressive, bold behavior. This attitude causes men to discriminate against women in the workplace. Until recently, women could not hold important positions in government and business. Before 1958 they could not vote in presidential elections. Today, more and more women who live in cities are going to university and pursuing rewarding careers. Many wait until they are older to marry and have children.

(top right) Grandparents play an important part in raising children and teaching good manners.
(bottom right) This Native-Mexican mother carries her baby in a large shawl.
(below) In some Mexican families, several generations live together. This picture shows three generations.

Some Native-Mexican men still wear sombreros and serapes *(top left)*, whereas women wear traditional shawls called rebozos *(bottom left)*.

(top right) Fashionable modern clothing is common among young Mexicans.
*(bottom right) The **charro** is worn by some performers.*

Clothes and costumes

Most Mexicans wear T-shirts and jeans, skirts and blouses, and pants and jackets. In rural areas, however, many Native Mexicans still wear traditional clothing. Festival days are occasions for dressing in colorful costumes.

Native clothing

Traditional Native clothing is made of hand-woven cotton cloth embroidered with wool in colorful designs. Clothing styles differ among the many different Native groups.

A rural man might wear cotton pants that come to just below the knees. His *guayabera*, a pale-colored loose cotton shirt, is worn beltless over the pants. A wool *poncho* or *serape* keeps him warm on chilly nights. Thick-soled sandals called *huaraches* protect his feet from thorns and sharp rocks.

His wife or daughter likely wears a *huipile*, which is a sacklike white cotton dress trimmed with brightly colored embroidered flowers. She wraps a shawl called a *rebozo* around her shoulders when she goes into the village or has visitors. Women of the Huave Native group wear a red sash around their waists.

Costumes

On fiesta days, many people wear colorful and decorative costumes. Both men and women don the costume of the *charro*—a Mexican rodeo performer who does tricks on horseback. This spectacular costume is studded with gold and silver and is topped by a large sombrero with a specially shaped brim.

The useful sombrero

The **sombrero** is a useful item for many rural farmers because it protects their faces from the burning sun. When people think of Mexican sombreros, they often imagine tall hats with huge turned-up brims. In the state of Morelos, sombreros have the famous large brims, but these hats differ from region to region. The sombreros of the Huichol people have flat crowns, medium-sized brims, and are decorated with brightly colored feathers. Yucatán farmers are famous for their braided palm-leaf sombreros.

China poblana

The national costume of Mexican women is named for a legendary princess who was famous for her generosity and good deeds. The *china poblana* consists of a full red-and-green skirt decorated with sequins and beads, an embroidered short-sleeved white blouse, and a silk shawl. It is worn by some women on patriotic holidays and at fancy balls.

The lively colors of the **china poblana** *make it a favorite costume among Mexican women.*

Religions and beliefs

In 1857 the Mexican government passed laws to separate the Roman Catholic church from the Mexican government. Before this time, the two had worked together and created laws about marriage, education, and justice. Today, **civil law**, or the law of the government, is the only recognized law in Mexico. Many people, however, still respect and obey religious laws as well.

Freedom of religion

The Mexican constitution guarantees everyone the right to follow the religion of his or her choice. Though most Mexicans are Roman Catholic, small communities of Protestants, Jews, and free-thinkers live in Mexico. **Mennonites**, a Christian group that does not believe in war, came to Mexico over one hundred years ago to escape religious oppression in Europe.

Roman Catholics

Almost all Mexicans belong to the Roman Catholic faith, but Mexican Catholics still practice some of their Native ways. The result is an interesting blend of religious customs. During Lent, the period of forty days before Easter, most Catholics **abstain** from, or give up, their favorite things. Mexican Catholics, however, choose to celebrate Lent with singing, dancing, and feasting.

Day of Our Lady of Guadalupe

In Mexico, December 12 is the most important Catholic holiday of the year. On the "Day of Our Lady of Guadalupe," over six million Catholics from Mexico and other countries travel to her shrine, La Villa, in Mexico City. In cities and villages around the country, Mexicans wake up early and rush out of their homes to the town square. A big party is about to take place! It will last the whole day and night. Colorful balloons and flags are everywhere. Parades, *mariachi* bands, dancing, and fireworks are part of the event. The "Day of Our Lady of Guadalupe" celebrates the vision of a Native Mexican who believed that Mary, the mother of Jesus Christ, appeared and spoke to him.

Native beliefs

Mexico's tiny Native population still practices traditional religious rituals. Some Mayan groups worship ancient tribal gods called *Yuntzilobs*. Many Native Mexicans believe that pregnant women should not look at an eclipse of the sun or moon. If they do, harm might come to their babies. Although they developed in different places, Native religions and Catholicism share similarities. Like Catholics, Native Mexicans practice forms of confession, baptism, and fasting.

(above) Mayan Catholics attend mass in a rural church.
(left) Mennonites lead simple, traditional lives.
(below) On the "Day of the Dead," Mexicans leave offerings of food. This celebration honors dead family members.
(opposite page) Some Catholics approach the church on their knees to show humility.

  # On the farm

More than half the farmers in Mexico own land under the *ejido* system. An *ejido* is a farm shared by several families. In one type of *ejido*, each family is given a small plot of land for farming. The family is allowed to use or sell the crops it grows but, until recently, it could not sell the land. In another type of *ejido*, everyone works on one very large tract of land and shares the profits at harvest time. Unfortunately, *ejidos* are not very profitable. Farmers blame this lack of profit on poor soil and old equipment.

Humble homes

Three generations often live in a rural Mexican home that is the size of a two-car garage. One- or two-room houses are built of **adobe** brick, which is made of dried clay. These adobe homes have no electricity or dependable water supply. Family members sleep on straw mats called *petates*, which are spread out over the hard dirt floors. Women prepare food on a *metate*—a smooth stone that is used as a kitchen counter.

Although they lead simple lives, Mexican farmers do not call themselves poor. Instead, farm people with little money will say that they are *humilde* (humble). Their homes are cheerfully decorated with flowers and handmade crafts.

Praying for rain

Although most farmers use modern farming techniques, many also believe that prayer can make the difference between good and bad crops. Most farmers grow corn, which requires a great deal of rain. The rainy season begins in late May and ends in September. If rain has not fallen by June, farm communities bring out statues of Catholic saints and pray to them to bring rain. Some of the older Native farmers even pray to Tlaloc, an ancient rain god. If it has not rained by July, farmers can be seen shaking their statues in frustration! If there is still no rain by September, farmers search their souls to understand what they have done to deserve such a severe punishment.

Emiliano's farm

Emiliano is a farmer in the state of Morelos. His mother named him after Emiliano Zapata, the revolutionary leader from Morelos who fought for the peasants' right to own land. His farm is ten acres in size. In a few months he hopes to see most of it covered in corn. He and his wife Maria have two sons—Roberto and Carlos. Roberto, the oldest, moved to Mexico City last year to work in a factory. Emiliano is glad that his son was able to find a job; many of his friends' sons have not been as lucky. He is happy to have Carlos help him, but he knows that his youngest son will also have to leave home soon.

This morning Emiliano and Carlos wake up early to begin plowing. Maria prepares a breakfast of tortillas, beans, and sweet dark coffee. As Carlos readies the team of horses, Emiliano wonders whether this year's crop will be successful. Last year the rain did not come, and the crops failed. It was a hard winter, but Roberto helped by sending money home.

While her husband and son are in the fields, Maria works hard. In the morning she makes tortillas and puts together a lunch, which she takes to Emiliano and Carlos in the fields. In the afternoon, she tends a small vegetable garden and feeds the chickens and pigs. She hopes that there will be enough money this year to send Carlos to university—he wants to become a doctor.

At the end of the day, Emiliano and Carlos return home very tired. Maria has prepared tortillas with beans, pork, and tomatoes. She has added lots of chili peppers because Emiliano likes his food spicy. In the evening Maria and Emiliano discuss the future. He would like to buy a new horse this year, but Maria convinces him that saving for Carlos's future is more important. They go to bed early, falling asleep to the sound of crickets chirping in the fields.

(opposite page, left) Mexican farmers live in modest homes that blend into the surrounding landscape.
(opposite page, right) Fences keep cattle and other livestock from wandering away.
(left) Farm kitchens are simple and practical.
(below) Most farmers lack the money to buy modern farming equipment. A great deal of work must be done by hand.

🎩 Village life 🎩

The Mexican countryside is dotted with many small villages. Some are drab and dingy clusters of farmhouses, whereas others are colorful and pretty. No matter how different they might appear, most villages have two features in common: a central plaza and a marketplace.

A place to gather

A **plaza** is a small tree-filled park paved with flagstones and lined with benches. It is the heart of the village, where fiestas and celebrations take place. There is always lots of activity. The town hall and the largest church in the village can usually be found on the border of the plaza.

A place to haggle

The marketplace is located near the plaza in a large building that looks like a warehouse. Inside, vendors at small stands sell pineapples, mangos, watermelons, tomatoes, meat, and dairy products. Outside the marketplace building, other vendors sell everything imaginable, including fruits and vegetables, digital watches, medicinal teas, T-shirts, and traditional handicrafts.

Bargaining, or **haggling**, is an important part of doing business at the market. Mexican vendors would be very disappointed if a customer did not

try to convince them to lower their prices. Haggling over a price can often get very loud, but it is always considered fun. Mexican homemakers often boast about their haggling skills to friends and neighbors.

Market day

Though the marketplace is open every day, the busiest day is Sunday, when local farm families flock to the village. Market day is a good time for friends and family to get together and talk. After the market closes, people gather in the plaza, where a band plays.

The *paseo*

Although the *paseo* tradition has died out in the cities, people in rural villages still practice this old Mexican tradition. On Sunday evenings,

unmarried girls parade clockwise around the plaza, as the young men walk counter-clockwise. If a boy wants to become acquainted with a girl, he asks her if he can walk with her. Walking together can lead to dating. Walking hand in hand during the *paseo* is a couple's way of announcing that they are in love.

(top and opposite page) The plaza and marketplace are the heart of village life. Rural families look forward to the weekly visit to the market, where they can see a variety of foods, crafts, and unusual treats.

Nearly 30 percent of Mexico's population lives in the country's three largest cities: Mexico City, Guadalajara, and Monterrey. These cities resemble other modern cities around the world with their skyscrapers, sports stadiums, tree-filled parks, fancy restaurants, and fashionable boutiques.

Air pollution

Air pollution is so thick in Mexico's major cities that sometimes it hurts to breathe. Each year, thousands of people get sick from diseases caused by air pollution. Mexico City is one of the most polluted cities in the world. The pollution is due to the many factories around the city and the millions of cars that clog the city streets. Sometimes the pollution looks like heavy fog. Wealthy people are fortunate because they can afford to visit the countryside on weekends and breathe fresh air. Most city dwellers must breathe the smog every day.

Too many cars!

Mexico's cities have many cars, but not enough roads! Driving a car downtown is even slower than walking because there are so many traffic jams. Weaving through block after block of idling cars, street vendors sell motorists everything from newspapers to on-the-spot car washes!

Traveling underground

In the 1960s Mexico began building its first subway system, called the Métro. Today, it is one of the finest underground transportation systems in the world. Trains on the Métro can whisk people across the city quickly, quietly, and very inexpensively. The walls at each station are beautifully decorated with statues and paintings. While digging the subway, workers at the Piño Suárez station discovered the ruins of an Aztec temple. Now Piño Suárez is not just a subway station—it is also a mini-museum!

Life of luxury

Most wealthy Mexicans make their homes in the cities. Whether they have luxurious apartments or large houses, they live comfortable lives. Their modern homes have television sets, satellite dishes, and swimming pools. Servants look after their children, clean their homes, and tend their gardens.

The middle class

There is little good, affordable housing in Mexico's larger cities, so many middle-class Mexicans live in the smaller Spanish colonial cities. Colonial houses are built around central courtyards, which are shared by several families. These older homes are very beautiful, with balconies and decorative archways. The larger houses are divided into apartments, allowing several families to live under the same roof. They share washing and cooking facilities.

Slums and shanties

Every major city in Mexico is surrounded by low-grade housing. The **shantytown** around Mexico City covers hundreds of acres. The people who live there endure pollution, crime, and unsanitary conditions. Their houses are made of planks, plastic sheeting, and corrugated tin. Some Mexicans do not even have a shanty. At night, homeless people cover themselves with their *serapes* and huddle together in doorways.

(opposite page, top left) Large families crowd into tiny one-room shacks made of tin and plywood. Thousands of these makeshift homes surround Mexico's big cities.
(opposite page, circle) Many people do not have homes. They must live and sleep on the busy city streets.
(opposite page, top right) Street children try to earn money by selling jewelry and other items.
(opposite page, bottom) Some city-dwelling Mexicans are fortunate to live in beautiful homes.

Language and education

Spanish is the most commonly spoken language in Mexico. Until recently, however, many remote communities of Native Mexicans resisted learning this language. Over fifty Native languages are still spoken, but more and more people are learning to speak Spanish. They want to get good jobs and fit into the Spanish-speaking Mexican society. Today, Mexican children who grow up in tribal areas call the Native languages "Grandma's tongue."

Growing literacy

After the 1910 revolution, hundreds of schools opened all over Mexico, and millions of people learned to read and write. Movies also played an important part in helping Mexicans learn to read. Many Mexican people love movies, especially American movies. In the 1950s the Mexican government made a law requiring all foreign movies to have **subtitles** rather than **dubbing**. This meant that, instead of hearing the Spanish translations of English, the viewers had to read the Spanish words on the bottom of the screen in order to follow the story. Thanks to this and other useful programs, eight out of ten Mexicans can read and write today.

School for everyone

The Mexican government spends more money on education than most other Latin American countries. Public education is free for children from ages six to sixteen, and all children must go to school. Some parents pay to send their children to preschool for

(above) A game with blocks teaches these children the alphabet. Their private school provides them with an excellent education.

(above) Good behavior is important. Schoolchildren line up before going home at the end of the day.
(below) Dancing in very important in Mexico. In school, children learn traditional folk dances, such as the sword dance.

two years before they start *primaria* (primary school), which lasts six years. Primary-school children begin their school day at 8 a.m. and stay in class until 2 p.m., with a mid-morning snack break. After a late lunch, the afternoons are used for extra classes or sports.

After primary school, students go to *secundaria* (high school) for another three years, then *preparatoria* (college preparatory school) for four more years. Some high schools and college preparatory schools are run by the Roman Catholic church. Parents pay fees to send their children to these private schools, which provide a better preparation for university.

Higher education

Mexico has more than 300 professional schools, including universities, teacher-training colleges, and technical schools. Every year, over half a million young people earn a post-secondary degree or diploma. Education allows Mexico to remain an important country in world trade and technology and helps young people get good jobs.

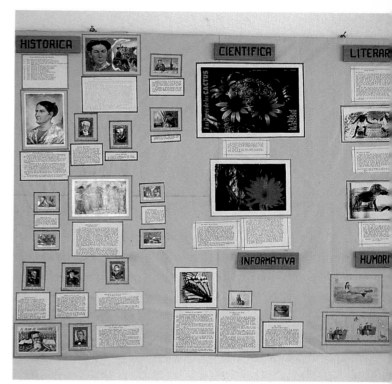

(top) **This bulletin board gives students a glimpse of what they will be studying.**
(bottom) **Over 100,000 students attend the National University of Mexico. Founded in 1551 by Charles V of Spain, it is the oldest university in North America.**

Pronouncing Spanish

Unlike the English and French languages, every single letter is sounded in Spanish.

- The letter **j** is pronounced **h**. For example, the name "Juan" sounds like "hwan."
- The letter **c** is hard, as in "cat." Upper-class Mexicans sometimes pronounce it **th**.
- The letter **z** is also pronounced **th**.
- Double **l** is pronounced like the letter **y**. The Spanish word for castle, *castillo*, is pronounced "cas-TEE-yoh."
- The letter **g** is always hard, as in "go," never soft, as in "giraffe."
- When you see the letters **qu**, they are not pronounced **kw** as in "quiet." Instead, they sound like the letter **k**. The Spanish word "que," meaning "what," is pronounced "kay."
- The letter **e** at the end of words is not silent. It is pronounced "ay," as in guacamole (gwa-cah-MO-lay).

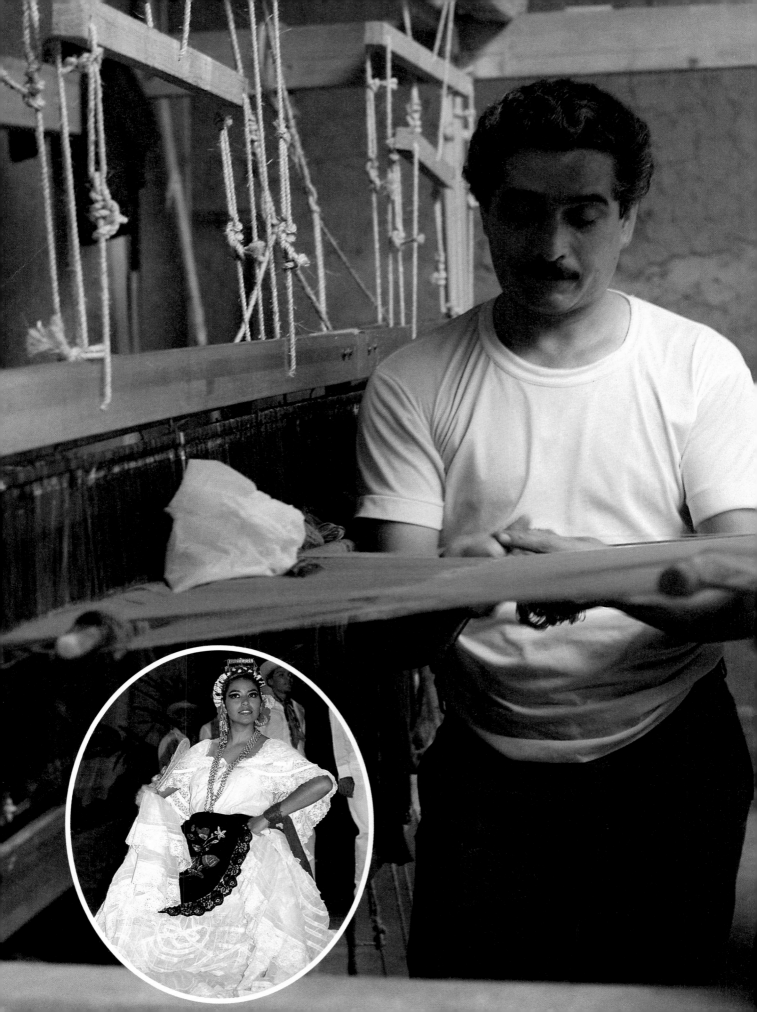

Mexicans at work

With such a huge population, Mexico's best resource is its people! One-third of all Mexicans work on the land as farmers. Many people fish in the country's lakes and coastal waters, using modern and traditional methods. Some Mexicans are doctors, scientists, and teachers. Others are writers, actors, and artisans. Factories are filled with men and women who manufacture high-tech items such as television sets and automobiles. No matter what their occupation, Mexicans have a reputation for being hard workers.

(above) This fresh-air barber shop is open for business!
(circle) Many Mexicans earn a living by fishing in the waters around the country.
(left) Mexican artisans, such as this papercutter, have a reputation for quality crafts.
(opposite page) Weavers use skills that have been passed down from the ancient Maya!
(opposite page, inset) This dancer entertains many tourists who visit her country.

27

Mexico's heroes

Mexicans have a long tradition of celebrating the people they admire through songs, stories, and poems. Some heroes are important historical figures, whereas others are artists and athletes. Who are your heroes? Write a song, poem, or story about your hero. Explain what this person has done and why you admire him or her.

"Perish the Spaniards"

On September 16, Mexicans celebrate Independence Day and honor Father Miguel Hidalgo y Costilla. Father Hidalgo was the leader of the 1810 rebellion against the Spanish. With the slogan "Perish the Spaniards," Father Hidalgo led an army of 80,000 Mexicans to regain Mexico's freedom.

The Mayor's Wife

María Josefa Ortiz de Domínguez is another hero of the 1810 rebellion. She was the wife of the mayor of Querétaro and a strong believer in Mexican independence. Risking great danger, she managed to pass a message to Father Hidalgo, telling him that the government had heard of the planned rebellion. Knowing the authorities were coming, Father Hidalgo and his followers were able to get away. Doña (Mrs.) Josefa was a brave woman who is still remembered today. Her face appears on Mexican coins and paper money. Her statue, called La Corregidora (The Mayor's Wife), stands in Mexico City.

The Savior of Mexico

Every year on March 21, the people of Mexico celebrate the birthday of Benito Juárez—"the Savior of Mexico." Juárez was a Zapotec and the first Native president of Mexico. From 1857 to 1872, Juárez created new laws and programs to protect human rights and help less-privileged Mexicans. He is sometimes called "the Abraham Lincoln of Mexico." Abraham Lincoln was the American president who freed African Americans from slavery.

For many Mexicans, Emiliano Zapata is a hero who represents the struggle for equality and dignity. Along with other revolutionaries, Zapata fought for the rights of less-privileged Mexicans.

Revolutionary heroes

When a ruthless general named Victoriano Huerta seized control of the Mexican government in 1910, the Mexican people began a civil war. Two of the most famous revolutionary leaders were Emiliano Zapata and Pancho Villa. Their slogan was "Land and Liberty" because they wanted both for the Mexican peasants. Today, Zapata and Villa are remembered in patriotic books, songs, and movies.

An inspiring woman

In the seventeenth century, a Mexican nun named Sister Juana Inès de la Cruz was famous for her writing. Her poetry is considered among the finest ever written in the Spanish language. Over the last 40 years, Mexican women have fought for equal rights. Many women admire Sister Inès, who inspired Mexican women to follow their dreams.

Sports legend

Like other North Americans, Mexicans love *béisbol, or* baseball. The first great baseball player to come from Mexico was a man named Bobby Avila. He played with the Cleveland Indians during the 1950s. Avila is a national hero. After he retired from baseball, he became an important Mexican politician. Today, Bobby Avila is a legend and role model for many young Mexicans.

Super Barrio

In 1985, a terrible earthquake hit Mexico City and caused the deaths of over 9000 people. Many people blamed the deaths on poorly constructed buildings. On June 12, 1987, huge crowds gathered to protest poor housing standards in front of a government building. Suddenly, fireworks exploded overhead, and a masked man appeared, wearing red tights, a long cape, and the letters "SB" on his chest.

No one knows the true identity of Super Barrio but, since 1987, many men dressed as Super Barrio have fought for the rights of the Mexican people. They campaign against pollution, poor working conditions, and the unfair treatment of women and the elderly.

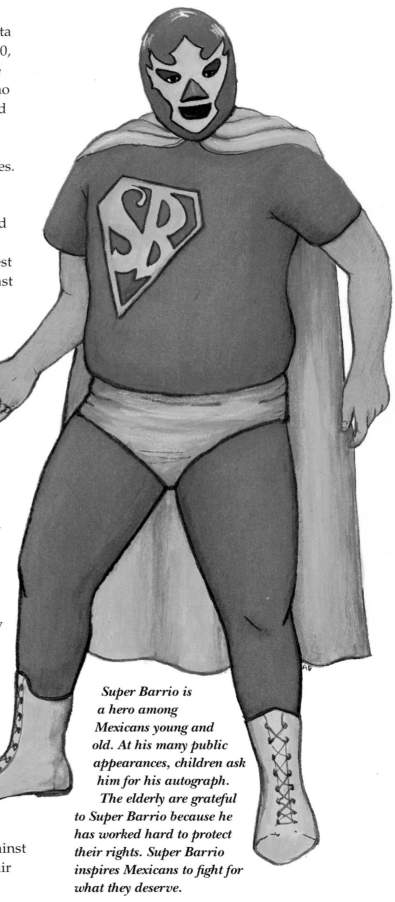

Super Barrio is a hero among Mexicans young and old. At his many public appearances, children ask him for his autograph. The elderly are grateful to Super Barrio because he has worked hard to protect their rights. Super Barrio inspires Mexicans to fight for what they deserve.

The future of Mexicans

Mexico is a land of opposites. Some resources, such as fish, seem unlimited, whereas others, such as forests, are quickly disappearing. High-tech manufacturing occurs not far from where Mexican Native peoples practice centuries-old traditions. The very rich live alongside people who live in extremely poor conditions.

Reasons for concern

People wonder how much longer Mexico can continue to support its quickly growing population and the increasing number of people who live in poverty. Some worry about what will happen to the country's huge population if Mexico's natural resources are used up. Many fear that the old ways will not survive in the face of modern technology. Environmental problems are also a growing cause for anxiety.

The government

The Mexican government is trying to help people. Though Mexico has an enormous foreign debt, it keeps the prices of staple foods such as tortillas, beans, and rice low, so that people can afford nutritious food. Mexico also has a government-run health-care system, which assures people of receiving proper, affordable health care. The government hopes that a free-trade agreement with the United States and Canada will provide more jobs for Mexicans.

. . . and the people

The Mexican people have survived for thousands of years—through conquests, revolutions, and natural disasters. They believe that the continued strength of their people, their religious faith, and preservation of their family values will guide them into the future.

Glossary

ancestors The people from whom one is descended

astronomy The study of the stars and planets

baptism The ceremony that shows a person has become a Christian

boar A type of wild pig

canals Artificial rivers that link larger bodies of water

charity An organization that helps the less fortunate

civil war A war that occurs between two groups within a country

class system A way of organizing society according to wealth or power

colonial Describing a land or people ruled by a distant country

confession The act of telling your sins to a priest and making amends

constitution A document that states the laws of a country

corrugated Having a grooved surface

discriminate To treat unfairly because of race, religion, or gender

eclipse The darkening of a sun, moon, or planet. On earth, this occurs when the moon comes directly between the earth and the sun, or when the earth comes between the sun and the moon.

embroider To decorate fabric with colorful needlework

enchilada A tortilla filled with meat or cheese

fasting Abstaining from food for a period of time

fiesta A Mexican celebration

flagstone A large, flat stone

flan A molded custard dessert with caramel sauce

free thinker An individual who does not belong to an organized religion

guacamole A dip made from avocadoes

homemaker A person who manages a household

immigrant A person who moves from one country to another

Latin America The Spanish- or Portugese-speaking countries south of the United States

literacy The ability to read and write

mango A tropical fruit

mariachi **band** A small band composed of a singer, violinist, guitarist, horn player, and bass player

mass A Christian ceremony which remembers the death and resurrection of Jesus Christ

metropolis A large, important city

moat A deep ditch surrounding a building, usually for the purpose of protection

nun A woman who has dedicated her life to God

orphan A person with no parents

plantation A large farm that specializes in one type of crop

post secondary Describing education after high school

promenade An unhurried walk

rainforest A dense forest that receives a great deal of rainfall

revolution A war in which people in a country fight against those in power

ritual An act performed regularly, often for religious reasons

Roman Catholic church The organization of Christians headed by the pope

rural Describing or relating to the countryside

saint A person recognized for his or her holiness

shanty A small, poorly built house

slogan A saying used by many people

standards Levels of quality set down as a guide or model

staple food The main food eaten by a people

suburbs The residential area around a city

subway An underground train system

tortilla A flat, thin bread made from cornmeal

vendor A salesperson, usually one who works on the street

Yucatán Describing the large Mexican peninsula that juts into the Caribbean Sea

Zapotec Describing or relating to a certain Native group from southern Mexico

Index

3 4 5 6 7 8 9 0   Printed in U.S.A.   2 1 0 9 8 7 6 5 4